100 QUESTIONS

about SPIES

and all
the answers
too!

Written and Illustrated by
Simon Abbott

PETER PAUPER PRESS, INC.
White Plains, New York

PETER PAUPER PRESS

In 1928, at the age of twenty-two, Peter Beilenson began printing books on a small press in the basement of his parents' home in Larchmont, New York. Peter—and later, his wife, Edna—sought to create fine books that sold at "prices even a pauper could afford."

Today, still family owned and operated, Peter Pauper Press continues to honor our founders' legacy of quality, value, and fun for big kids and small kids alike.

Designed by Heather Zschock

Published by Peter Pauper Press, Inc.
202 Mamaroneck Avenue
White Plains, New York 10601 USA

Published in the United Kingdom and Europe by Peter Pauper Press, Inc.
c/o White Pebble International
Unit 2, Plot 11 Terminus Rd.
Chichester, West Sussex PO19 8TX, UK

Library of Congress Cataloging-in-Publication Data

Names: Abbott, Simon, 1967- author, illustrator.
Title: 100 questions about spies : and all the answers too / written and
illustrated by Simon Abbott.
Other titles: One hundred questions about spies
Description: White Plains, New York : Peter Pauper Press, Inc., 2020. |
Series: 100 questions | Audience: Ages 7+ | Audience: Grades K-1 |
Summary: "This illustrated children's book examines the history of
international espionage through a series of questions and answers.
Subjects covered include descriptions of actual spy gadgets, discussions
of actual spy techniques, and famous spies in each major period of
history from the ancient Egypt and Greece to the Cold War"-- Provided by
publisher.
Identifiers: LCCN 2020018819 | ISBN 9781441334367 (hardcover)
Subjects: LCSH: Spies--History--Juvenile literature. |
Espionage--History--Juvenile literature.
Classification: LCC JF1525.I6 A24 2020 | DDC 327.1209--dc23
LC record available at https://lccn.loc.gov/2020018819

ISBN 978-1-4413-3436-7
Manufactured for Peter Pauper Press, Inc.
Printed in Hong Kong

7 6 5 4 3 2 1

WELCOME

to the undercover world of spies
and secret agents!

Let's search through top-secret
files and investigate gizmos, gadgets,
and daring disguises!

**Which spymaster was responsible
for a queen losing her head?**

What is a double agent?

**Why was a pigeon awarded a bravery
medal in World War II?**

How can I devise my own secret code?

Remember, this is classified information,
so let's keep things hush-hush!

I-SPY!

Let's get the inside track on the secretive spy world.

We'll start with the basics. What is a spy?
A spy gets information. Another word for this is espionage (*ES-pe-oh-naj*).

Are a secret agent and a spy the same thing?
Secret agents are hired, usually by an agency, to collect information. A spy is *anyone* who collects information, including people who analyze it or sell it to others.

Do spies only operate during wartime?
It's true that military secret agents are busy in wartime, getting classified information on an enemy's plans, technology, and weaponry. In peacetime, a government spy works undercover to gather intelligence on their opponents, and an industrial or corporate spy tries to get the heads up on a business rival's secrets.

So a spy's job is to get hold of information. How can they do this?
Spies gather intelligence in many ways. Let's see how many you've heard of!

Human Intelligence (HUMINT)
Collecting info from human sources, such as interviewing a witness, or listening in on a phone call.

Signals Intelligence (SIGINT)
Tapping into electronic transmissions (calls, texts, emails, etc.) from offices, satellites, ships, or planes. Intercepting signals between two operatives is known as communications intelligence (COMINT).

Imagery Intelligence (IMINT)
Data gathered from photos. These could be taken by secret cameras or satellites out in space.

Open-source Intelligence (OSINT)
Information available to everyone, such as newspapers, radio and TV broadcasts, or government reports.

What are the most effective ways for a spy to uncover secret info?
One of the best ways to snoop on your enemy is to worm your way into (or infiltrate) their organization. You may need a disguise, or a brand-new identity, to do this. Once inside, you can send information, or intelligence, to your bosses and sniff out rebel operatives within the organization who might help you with classified scoops.

What do you call an undercover tarantula?

A spy-der!

How else could a spy discover insider information?
Let's take a look at some of the top tools and techniques:

Spy Cameras
Operatives can snoop on their targets with tiny cameras disguised in bags, pens, and watches.

Bugs
These are listening devices that can be discreetly hidden in plant pots, wall sockets, and even inside credit cards!

Spy Tracking Devices
A target can be located with a tracking device, which can be fixed to an individual, a vehicle, or heavy-duty equipment.

Computer Hacking
Agents can obtain secret digital data using cyber spy technology to hack into computer systems and smart phones.

Coded Messages
Spies have used a huge variety of methods to sneak information back to their headquarters. Messages have been sent as knitting patterns, newspaper advertisements, and even written using invisible ink!

THE HISTORY OF SPIES: EARLY DAYS

It's time to flick through the history books and look at the spy world's starting point.

Isn't spying a modern-day method of slick surveillance? How far back do we need to go?

Well, spying is mentioned many times in the Bible, with various groups within the tribes of Israel snooping on each other. The ancient Greeks, Egyptians, and Romans all established spy networks to help grow their empires.

How do we know this?

Have you heard of Egyptian **hieroglyphs** (*HI-roh-glifs*)? This is an ancient writing system, and scrolls inscribed with these symbols reveal stories from the ancient past. These writings show that early Egyptian rulers used agents to spy on rebel subjects or tribes. Spies used secret codes, invisible inks, and hidden compartments in their robes, and developed the use of poisons to assassinate their opponents.

Which other ancient civilizations developed espionage techniques?
The ancient Greeks were trailblazers in their development of military intelligence.
Secrets were uncovered by spies disguised as house slaves, refugees, or army
deserters. This info was transmitted back to headquarters by methods such as
secret codes in letters, and messages in the sole of a spy's sandal, engraved on an
earring, or written on an inflated animal bladder and then concealed in a water
flask. Messages were hidden in dog collars or attached to arrows, and codes were
even drilled into sheep bones. These super-smart secret agents even developed
early decoding machines!

**That's a bit sneaky! What other top-secret techniques did the ancient
Greeks figure out?**
Spies were used to get the inside track on the size of a rival's army, or the strength
of their defenses. This classified information was communicated between cities
by signaling towers using a device called the **hydraulic telegraph**. Those skillful
secret agents!

Did any ancient Greeks go above and beyond the call of duty?
Spare a thought for the slave of the bully **Histiaeus**. This sneaky ruler wanted to
send confidential information to his son-in-law, so he shaved his slave's hair and
had the message tattooed on the man's shiny bald head. Once his hair had
regrown, the slave was dispatched, with the instruction to shave his head once
more when he arrived at his destination. The secret message was then revealed!

7

Rome was famous for its armies, but what about its spy network?
It's true that the ancient Roman army was a superior fighting force. However, it also relied on a number of undercover agents, whose tactics included disguising themselves as peasants to gather information behind enemy lines.

What tactics did the Romans' enemies use?
Hannibal, the Carthaginian leader, surprised the Roman army with his undercover methods of disguise, forgery, and secret communication. His spies identified each other through secret hand signals, but had to watch out if they were captured. One of Hannibal's agents was caught in the act, and the Romans cut off his hands, then released him back to the enemy as a warning to other spies.

What can other ancient civilizations teach us about spying?
Sun Tzu was a Chinese military expert who wrote a book called *The Art of War* about 2,500 years ago. In it, he details the importance of spies and espionage in wartime. As one of history's greatest military brains, Sun Tzu inspired army training for thousands of years.

Sounds impressive! What did he write about spies?
Quite a bit! For example:

"The enemy's spies who have come to spy on us must be sought out, tempted with bribes, led away and comfortably housed. Thus, they will become converted spies and available for our service."

Well, he sounds like a sensible fellow. Was all his writing so merciful?
Not so fast! Check out this bit of military advice:

"If a secret piece of news is divulged by a spy before the time is ripe, he must be put to death together with the man to whom the secret was told."

Gulp!

So, was Sun Tzu correct? Are spies essential to military dominance?
Genghis Khan would probably agree. In 1206 he started the **Mongol Empire**, which at its peak covered an enormous 12 million square miles (31 million sq km). By comparison, the USA covers about 3.8 million square miles (9.8 million sq km). He established networks of spies, who spent months before a military attack investigating defenses, mapping out tracks, planning escape routes, scouting out supplies, and more. As Genghis Khan is supposed to have said, "A man's greatest joy is crushing his enemies." (This was before pizza was invented!)

THE HISTORY OF SPIES: TUDOR TIMES

Let's fast-forward to the 1500s and expose the spies and secret agents hiding in the shadows. First stop . . . Venice!

We know that Venice was full of amazing architecture and art.
Are you saying it was also a secret agent hot-spot?
Back in a period of time called the Renaissance (1300–1500), Venice was a wealthy and influential city. Its location and powerful navy helped Venice become a major center for trade between Europe and the Middle East. The city's dominance in Italy led to disagreements and wars with its rivals. A spy network was needed!

What sort of spy network did Venice create?
Venice created one of the world's first state intelligence services, a bit like the CIA. Spy chiefs, known as the Council of Ten, masterminded the network of agents and code-breakers across departments, including operations, science, and technology. The Venetian secret service worked from its headquarters in the Ducal Palace, in St. Mark's Square.

How did the Venetian spymasters recruit their secret agents?
Merchants who traveled far and wide were enlisted to gather intelligence and report back. Venetian ambassadors around the world would recruit local operatives, and pay them in fine wines or fancy paintings. Even ordinary Venetians were encouraged to spill secret information. Mailboxes in the shape of a lion's mouth were installed around the city, and sneaky citizens wrote down and mailed any tips they picked up about threats to the city.

**Did spies in this period sneak around in the shadows,
wearing black cloaks and false beards?**
Let's take **Petrus Alamire** as an example. He was a magnificent musician, as well as (according to some reports) a mining engineer. He personally delivered his elaborate music manuscripts to royal palaces throughout Europe. This was a first-rate cover for a spy, and he was soon recruited by **King Henry VIII** of England. Henry was worried about the threat to his throne from Richard de la Pole, who lived in exile at the court of the French king, Louis XII. Alamire and his undercover network of musician friends were able to keep Henry VIII up-to-date on Pole's attempts to overthrow the king. Fortunately for Henry, Pole died at the Battle of Pavia in 1525, so his threat never took shape.

Was that the end of threats to the English throne?
No! Have you heard of Henry VIII's daughter, Queen Elizabeth I?
She ruled England for 44 years, and although she was impressive and popular,
there were many plots against her. Bring on the spy network!

Who were these Elizabethan undercover agents?
They were led by the queen's spymaster, **Francis Walsingham**. He was a
super-brainy, ruthless operator, and set up a spy school to train new recruits
in the art of coded messages, invisible ink, and skillfully lifting a wax seal
from a letter so that it could be secretly opened and read.

Who was Queen Elizabeth I's biggest threat?

Awkwardly, it was her cousin, Mary, Queen of Scots. Walsingham intercepted Mary's letters, decoded them, then resealed them. After waiting patiently for firm evidence, he finally discovered a letter that confirmed Mary's participation in a plot to overthrow Elizabeth. At Mary's trial, she attacked Walsingham's sneaky methods: "*Spies are men of doubtful credit,*" she announced, "*who make a show of one thing and speak another.*"

Was Mary found guilty?
Yes. After pressure from Walsingham, Queen Elizabeth I reluctantly signed her cousin's death warrant. Mary, Queen of Scots, was beheaded at Fotheringhay Castle in 1587.

DISGUISES, DOCUMENTS, AND DROP-OFFS

How can spies change their identities to blend in or gain entry to a secret organization? Let's look at these daring disguises!

What kinds of disguises are there?

A **light disguise** could be a simple pair of glasses, a wig, or a false beard. If you need to go deeper, you can use an **advanced disguise**, which may include a full-face mask, dental façades (false teeth), plumpers (covers for teeth that make cheeks look puffier), or other **prosthetics** (*PRAWS-theh-tiks*—or fake body parts) that change the way you look. They can change your apparent age, your gender, and even the way you speak!

What is the golden rule for a fool-proof disguise?

Remember: You're hiding in plain sight, which means you must be completely forgettable. How you act is just as important as how you look. How do you walk? How do you talk? How should you hold your knife and fork? What do the locals order in a coffee shop?

How long can a spy keep up a fake identity?

Elena Vavilova and **Andrei Bezrukov** were Russian spies who went undercover as a Canadian couple, taking the names Tracey Foley and Donald Heathfield, for 20 years. They even kept their identities secret from their children! They had endured long hours of language training to perfect North American accents, and had lived in a pretend American home built outside Moscow, to get themselves used to the U.S. As Elena said, "*A spy has to be an actor, but an actor that doesn't need a public or a stage.*"

How did spies conceal classified information?
If two agents needed to pass on secret intelligence, but didn't want to meet, they would arrange a **dead drop**, or a hiding place agreed upon by both agents, where secret objects (photos, instructions, recordings, etc.) sealed in special containers would be dropped off by one spy and picked up by the other. To tell the other agent that the hiding place contained something new, the person making the drop would use a signal that seemed ordinary, like chalk marks on a wall or window blinds turned a certain way. The container for the dead drop itself needed to be just as ordinary-looking, such as a spike pushed into the ground.

What other objects have been camouflaged in the world of espionage?
British spies once hid a multi-million-pound listening device on a Moscow street, disguised as a rock! Also in Moscow, just before the end of WWII, the Soviet Union's **All-Union Pioneer Organization** (basically, the Boy and Girl Scouts) presented a carved wooden plaque to the American ambassador, Averell Harriman. This gift contained a hidden listening device that transmitted the ambassador's conversations and phone calls for seven years.

How have secret documents been hidden?
Christopher Clayton Hutton, a member of Britain's MI5 agency, made maps printed on silk that he would hide inside objects like a playing card deck and a gramophone record. For the latter, soldiers would break the record to get at the map. This is why Hutton called this particular plan Operation Smash-Hit!

THE HISTORY OF SPIES: REVOLUTION IN AMERICA

It's the 1770s. The American colonies are fed up with paying taxes to the British king, George III, and want their independence! Bring on the Revolutionary War!

Did George Washington try to send spies behind enemy lines?
Yes. In 1776, Nathan Hale, a captain for the Continental (colonial) Army, volunteered to join the British army (pretending to be a Dutch schoolmaster) and gather information about plans and strategies. He was caught, thrown in jail, and sentenced to execution. His last words were, "*I only regret that I have but one life to give for my country.*"

What role did spies play in this war?
Who were the main players in the colonial intelligence network?
In 1778, George Washington asked Major Benjamin Tallmadge to set up a spy network near the British headquarters in New York City. Tallmadge formed the Culper Spy Ring, which was a network of merchants, tailors, farmers, and military officers who would pass on valuable intelligence about the British plans.

The Culper Spy Ring didn't have smartphones or laptops.
How did they communicate?
American patriot **Anna Smith Strong** would hang clothes and handkerchiefs in a certain order to tell colonial spies about messages and drop-off points. **Abraham Woodhull** pretended to be loyal to King George III. Using the spy name of **Samuel Culper**, he would listen in on British soldiers' conversations, then write down key information and tuck these notes away in isolated caves. Other spies would then pick up the notes from their hiding places.

16

How did Woodhull prevent his messages from being read by the British?
Woodhull wrote his reports in a valuable disappearing ink. One night, when
he was writing a secret message, Woodhull's nieces burst into the room to
surprise him. Thinking they were British officers, he quickly grabbed the papers
and smashed the bottle of special ink on the floor. George Washington sent
him a replacement bottle immediately!

What other spy inventions were used?
Future U.S. president Thomas Jefferson invented a **wheel cipher**, which
was a device that encoded and decoded messages. Although Jefferson gave
up on the gadget in the 1800s, a copycat machine was later developed
and used by the military right up until World War II.

Did any spies act as double-agents?
James Armistead Lafayette, an enslaved African American man in Virginia, joined
the patriot army. He was sent undercover to British camps, and posed as a runaway
slave to gather information. There, he gained the trust of the general Benedict
Arnold, who had left the Continental Army for the British. Enemy officers talked
about strategies in front of Armistead, and he wrote detailed reports which were
passed back through the spy network to his boss, General Lafayette of the Continental Army. His information led to Washington's victory at Yorktown in 1781—the
battle that decided the Revolutionary War. After the war, James asked the Virginia
Assembly for his freedom. A letter from his general explained the importance of
Armistead's work, and he became a free man in 1787.

17

THE HISTORY OF SPIES: WORLD WAR I

On August 4, 1914, Germany invaded Belgium, and the first World War (or WWI) began. Let's take a look!

How did spycraft change during WWI?

In previous wars, information about the enemy was usually gathered on the battlefield, with agents infiltrating enemy lines. Espionage during World War I needed a new approach, because of the length of the war and the fact that often neither side gained much ground. The new type of spying became known as the Secret War.

What innovations took place?

Britain was ahead of the game, as it had formed its Secret Service Bureau in 1909. Advances in flight and photography meant that agents could photograph the enemy's movements, positions, and weaponry from the air. The first aerial photography, though, came from pigeons carrying cameras that were deployed by the German military. Over the four years of the war, more than 250 spy networks were established among the countries that were allied against Germany and Austria-Hungary, including Britain, France, Russia, and the United States.

How did the agents pass on secret information?

Confidential messages were sent by radio and telegraph, and operatives called cryptographers (*CRIP-taw-gra-fers*) wrote and solved codes. The way they delivered messages had to be just as secretive. Britain sent maps to prisoners of war inside board games. Spies delivered reports on enemy movements to generals by attaching them to the legs of pigeons.

Who were some stand-out spies from the First World War?

The most famous agent was known as Mata Hari. Whether or not she was a competent spy is up for debate. She rubbed elbows with European military elites frequently. Because of this, German officials offered her money to spy for them, but she took the money and ran! Later, the French enticed her into spywork. As a French spy, Mata Hari tried to uncover what the German military was doing, but any attempts she made at sending intel back to France failed . . . because France was setting her up! Despite the fact that no one could prove she was spying for Germany, Mata Hari was arrested and then executed as a double-agent on October 15, 1917.

Edith Cavell worked covertly for the British, and using her cover as a nurse, helped at least 200 French, British, and Belgian soldiers to escape from German captivity.

WWI was a promising time for female agents. Sixteen-year-old Jane Sissmore joined the British secret service (MI5) as a secretary in 1916. By 1924, she had climbed through the ranks to become the organization's chief expert on Soviet affairs.

We've heard of the spy networks in mainland Europe. Did any German agents make it onto British soil?

Germany sent 120 spies into Great Britain to gather intelligence, but the British caught 65 of them. Some of these agents were poorly trained. One sent primitive codes hidden as import documents for sardines; he was caught because sardines were out of season. Two others used cigar shipments to send coded messages, and were also caught because British sailors didn't smoke cigars.

How about American soil?

Some German operatives traveled even farther afield. On July 30, 1916, German agents blew up a weapons factory on Black Tom Island in New York Harbor. This act of sabotage destroyed $20,000,000 of supplies, damaged the Statue of Liberty's torch, and led to the American army joining WWI the following year.

THE HISTORY OF SPIES: WORLD WAR II

Twenty-one years later, the world was at war once again.

World War II was a war between two groups of countries: the Allies, including Great Britain, France, the Soviet Union, China, and the U.S.; and the Axis powers of Germany (whose government was known as the Nazis), Italy, Japan, and others.

What was at the top of the British government's espionage to-do list?
The Enigma was a coding machine used by the Germans to send out secret messages. At the start of World War II, the British established a Code and Cipher School to try and break the Enigma code. This mission was made even harder when the Germans stepped up security and changed the code system every day!

That's impossible! Could anyone break that code?
Led by the brilliant mathematician Alan Turing, the British team invented a code-breaking machine called the Bombe. This allowed them to read German naval messages, guide Allied ships away from the enemy, and help win the Battle of the Atlantic. Their work saved countless lives, shortened the war by several years, and laid the foundations for modern computers.

What wartime cutting-edge technology made its way
into a secret agent's spy kit?
Let's take a look at some interesting inventions:

Exploding Chocolate
The British Secret Service uncovered a plot to assassinate
Prime Minister Winston Churchill with a bomb covered with a layer of
real chocolate. When a piece was broken off, the bomb would explode
seven seconds later.

Spy Pen
This seemingly everyday object could contain a secret map and
two compasses (one in the pen cap and the other in the pen clip).

Microdot
French and German spies would take photographs
of secret messages and reduce them to the size of this dot,
then hide them in ordinary messages. The recipient would
then enlarge the dot and read the secret information.

Which British spy really had the Germans fooled?
In April 1943, British agent William Martin was found drowned off the Spanish
coast, with a briefcase chained to his wrist. German forces were alerted, and pried
open the case to read the confidential documents inside. They were amazed to
discover British plans for an invasion of Sardinia and Greece. This seemed like a
major coup for the Germans, and their leader (or Führer), Adolf Hitler, sent thousands
of soldiers to Greece. But they'd been fooled. The documents were fake, and the
body was not William Martin, but rather the corpse of a predeceased homeless man.
Instead of Greece, the Allies invaded Sicily and Italy with 160,000 soldiers.

Who did the Germans call the "most dangerous of all allied spies"?
Let's hear it for **Virginia Hall**! With a false name and a forged passport, she traveled to occupied France posing as an American reporter. As an undercover agent for Britain, she recruited spies, radioed information on German military activity, and wrote news stories packed with coded messages for the spy chiefs in London. When the German Gestapo put up posters for her arrest, she escaped and fled 50 miles (80 km) on foot over the Pyrenees mountains to Spain. She wasn't done though. Working for the U.S., she returned to France in 1944 disguised as a 60-year-old peasant, then led a team that blew up bridges, derailed trains, and killed or captured 650 Nazis.

What a woman! What else makes Virginia Hall's story so remarkable?
She did all of this despite the fact that her left leg had been amputated! In its place, she wore a 7-pound (3 kg) wooden prosthetic that she named "Cuthbert." After the war, Hall was the only female WWII veteran to be awarded the **Distinguished Service Cross**, one of the highest honors of the U.S. military.

Which other agents went above and beyond?

Introducing the greatest double agent of WWII, **Juan Pujol**, code-named **GARBO**. He convinced the German high command that the Allies were intending to invade Europe in Calais, France. The invasion was true, but the actual landing was planned further south in Normandy. The MI5 supported this misinformation with "reports" of a fake American army preparing to launch from southeast England. GARBO's deception worked; Hitler moved two armored divisions and 19 infantry units to Calais, to face the Allied assault that never came.

What happened to GARBO once the troops invaded at Normandy and his deception was revealed?

GARBO sent urgent messages to German high command to instruct them that the Normandy invasion of 156,000 soldiers was just a diversion, and that the Calais assault would still take place. Hitler was convinced. In fact, he was so convinced that the German Führer awarded GARBO the Iron Cross, one of the highest military awards in Nazi Germany's army, for his "extraordinary" services.

Which WWII operative created the world's most famous fictional spy?

Ian Fleming was an agent for British Naval Intelligence and collected secret information coming in from around the world. He was promoted to commander and helped to establish Assault Unit 30, a top-secret intelligence-gathering commando crew. All of this was great material for the novels he went on to write, featuring the fictional spy **James Bond**.

THE HISTORY OF SPIES: THE COLD WAR

In the aftermath of WWII, the U.S. and Russia (then part of the Soviet Union) became the world's superpowers. Their tense power struggle became known as the Cold War. Read on!

Why was it called the Cold War? Was it because of the chilly Russian winters?
It was called the **Cold War** because the two countries never directly attacked each other. Both countries developed nuclear weapons and competed in an arms race to see who could stockpile the deadliest arsenal.

How did the superpowers become rivals? Weren't the U.S. and Russia allies in WWII?
Despite being on the same side at the end of World War II, they had competing beliefs. The U.S. believed in **capitalism** and **democracy**, where individuals can earn wealth free from government control. The Soviet Union, on the other hand, was **communist** and **authoritarian**, a system where all property (houses, money, even food) was owned by the government, to be distributed equally among its people.

Because the U.S. and the Soviet Union were becoming rival world leaders, they each scrambled to grab the most power across the globe. That meant convincing other countries not only to ally with them but also to adopt their ideas. This struggle for power and influence led the U.S. and Soviet Union to become bitter rivals for almost half a century.

Yikes! So how did these superpowers employ super-secret spywork?

During WWII, the Soviets had launched an all-out spying mission to discover American and British military secrets. So, these three countries created major spy networks within each other's countries.

COMMUNIST PARTY ORGANIZATION U.S.A. FEB. 9, 1950

A spy network at home? How did this affect day-to-day life?

Greatly! Starting shortly after WWII, the U.S. government's House Un-American Activities Committee (HUAC), designed to root out anyone who seemed disloyal to the U.S., stepped up their efforts. They claimed communists had worked their way into all aspects of American life. In 1950, Wisconsin senator Joseph McCarthy claimed that over 205 communists had infiltrated the American government. Between McCarthy and the HUAC, a witch hunt raged during the early years of the Cold War. This period of fear was known as the Second Red Scare. (The first took place between World Wars I and II.)

However, the Second Red Scare began to fade in 1954, when McCarthy took aim at Army war heroes and the American public turned against him. The public also stopped trusting the HUAC, which was further limited by the Senate. Aalthough the public condemned the witch hunts, the fear remained, and the government continued to monitor its own people for signs of communists throughout the Cold War.

What were some notable spy missions of the Cold War?
The Soviet Union was especially interested in the top-secret U.S. program to develop an atomic bomb, the **Manhattan Project**, which occurred way back during World War II. One of the key scientists was **Klaus Fuchs**, a German-born physicist who became a British citizen in 1942. He has been called "the most important atomic spy in history," as during WWII he passed information to the Soviets that enabled them to create their own atomic bomb. Post-world-war, this let the Soviet Union arm themselves just as heavily as the U.S. Fuchs secretly continued his spywork well into the Cold War, after he was offered a position at the UK's Atomic Energy Research Establishment.

Did Fuchs work alone?
There were networks of Soviet spies in the U.S. throughout the Cold War. **Julius Rosenberg** was a communist whose job at the Army Signal Corps Engineering Laboratory made him an effective Soviet spy. He began to work for the Russians and enlisted his brother-in-law **David Greenglass**, who worked alongside Fuchs on the Manhattan Project.

How was the spy ring discovered?
The U.S. developed a project called VENONA to decode encrypted Russian communications. The American cryptanalysts were stunned by what they read. Russian agents had infiltrated the State Department, the Treasury, the Office of Strategic Services, and even the White House!

Did the spy ring escape to Russia?
After being caught in 1949, Fuchs served nine years in a British jail, then moved to communist East Germany. Greenglass made a deal with the U.S. government. He was sentenced to a 15-year jail term, and in return for his wife's freedom, he accused his sister Ethel Rosenberg of spying right alongside her husband. Julius and Ethel Rosenberg later faced the electric chair, becoming the only U.S. civilian spies ever executed on American soil.

Were there any other spies outside of the U.S.?
Meet Harold "Kim" Philby. After WWII, he became head of Britain's MI6's anti-Soviet section, but secretly worked as a KGB agent at the same time. He was part of the **Cambridge Five** spy ring, a group of spies in high-ranking British government positions who passed information to the Russians during WWII and the Cold War. Although he was caught, he and the rest of the Cambridge Five were never jailed. Philby fled to Moscow, where instead of the hero's welcome he was expecting, he lived the rest of his life as a virtual prisoner to the Soviets.

With all these Soviet spies among American and British ranks,
was there a Russian spy on *our* side?
There were plenty, but perhaps the most notable one was **Dmitri Polyakov**, alias **TOP HAT**, a high-ranking official in the Soviet Union's branch of military intelligence, the GRU. As he rose through the ranks of the GRU, Polyakov grew to hate the corruption of the Soviet government, so he offered his services to the CIA. From 1961 to sometime in the 1980s, Polyakov passed valuable intel to the CIA. The massive amount of intelligence he gathered helped the U.S. stay one step ahead of the Soviet Union throughout the Cold War by strengthening relationships with Soviet allies (like China) and rooting out spies among their own ranks.

GADGETS AND GIZMOS

No secret agent's kit is complete without some deadly devices and an awesome apparatus or two. Let's see what's on a spy's wish list!

As we know, a spy should be able to hide in plain sight. Which everyday object has concealed a deadly purpose?

Among others, an umbrella! Georgi Markov was a critic of the communist Bulgarian government who feared for his safety and fled to London. He was standing at a bus stop on Waterloo Bridge when he suddenly felt a stinging pain in his leg. A stranger then dropped an umbrella, hailed a taxi, and fled the scene. Markov shrugged off the incident and continued his journey home. Three days later, Markov was dead, having been shot by the umbrella with a pinhead-sized pellet of a deadly poison.

What other household items should I stay away from?

In the 1960s, the Russian KGB developed a lipstick pistol, which could deliver the ultimate "kiss of death" by a simple twist of the tube. This could be a nice addition to the face powder compact, which revealed secret codes when its mirror was at a certain angle. And for use in cold weather, the U.S. Navy invented a glove gun in the 1940s, which would fire when an agent punched their victim.

I'm going undercover on a top-secret assignment.
How should I conceal my camera?

Cameras have been hidden in pens, cigarette lighters, and key chains. Secret meetings could be photographed with a Steineck wristwatch, and flash-free night-time pictures could be taken with infrared film hidden in a regular briefcase. First prize goes to the buttonhole camera. Spies would tuck the camera behind a coat button and take pictures by squeezing a cable in the coat pocket.

Which gadgets help agents spy from afar?
How about a fake cigar that turns into a **silent helicopter**? Just take the top off the cigar and hidden inside are rotating blades and a miniature camera.

Did James Bond's famous spy car actually exist?
Bond's car, the incredible **Aston Martin DB5** first driven in *Goldfinger*, came equipped with machine guns, oil jets, tire slashers, radar screen, bulletproof shields, rotating license plates, and a passenger ejector seat. Although the director of the CIA, Allen Dulles, and *James Bond* creator Ian Fleming were good friends, it's doubtful such a car ever existed in the real world. After all, a spy's job is to blend in, and the Aston Martin is hardly low-key!

Ever since WWI, spy planes have been used to get information about enemy forces. How did these aircraft develop?
Take a look at these pioneering American planes, whose mission was to gather intelligence with minimal detection:

NAME: SR-71 Blackbird
TOP SPEED: 2,193 mph (3,530 km/h)
That's nearly four times faster than a jumbo jet!
MAX ALTITUDE: 85,000 feet (25,908 m)

NAME: U-2 Dragon Lady
TOP SPEED:
500 mph (805 km/h)
ALTITUDE: 70,000 feet (21,336 m)

On May 1, 1960, one of these single-seater spy planes belonging to the American military was shot down as it flew over the Soviet Union. Pilot Gary Powers survived, but he was held in a prison camp for two years, until the Americans struck a deal with the Soviets to exchange him for KGB agent Rudolf Abel.

NAME: MQ-1B Predator
TOP SPEED:
135 mph (217 km/h)
ALTITUDE:
25,000 feet (7,620 m)

This unmanned aircraft is flown by a remote crew. It may be slow compared to other spy planes, but after gathering covert intelligence, it can strike immediately with its two laser-guided missiles.

How high does spying go?
Intelligence or reconnaissance satellites can be launched into space to take detailed photographs, listen in on communications, detect missile launches, and track military movements. In 2011, the American military launched a 23-story rocket from Vandenberg Air Force base in California to deliver a top-secret spy satellite into space. Experts believe that the satellite can take photos so detailed that you could recognize the make and model of an automobile hundreds of miles below.

HEROES, HEROINES, AND VICIOUS VILLAINS

Let's shine the spotlight on some renowned spies. How did their exploits earn them a place in the secret agent hall of fame?

CONFIDENTIAL

KARL SCHULMEISTER (1770–1853)

When did he start his career in espionage?
Although he began as an agent for Austria, he flipped sides and began spying for France during the Napoleonic Wars in 1804.

Was he a successful agent?
He was an excellent spy, and was described as having "all brains and no heart"! He convinced the Austrians that the French planned to retreat, and even went to the trouble of having fake French newspapers printed to back up his story. The French then surrounded the Austrian army and captured them all easily!

HARRIET TUBMAN (1822–1913)

Who was she?

From 1861 to 1865, the United States fought in a brutal Civil War, dividing itself between the Union North (anti-slavery, generally) and the Confederate South (pro-slavery). During this time, Tubman, a former slave, would venture into Confederate territory and gather information from enslaved people about the Confederate troops' plans, including where their soldiers had stashed barrels of gunpowder in order to attack Union boats.

What were her most important missions?

She was the first woman in U.S. history to lead an armed military expedition. In 1863, she led a raid along South Carolina's Combahee River, and freed over 700 enslaved people from nearby plantations. Before this, she made over 19 challenging journeys from the North to the South, using a network of secret routes called the Underground Railroad, to bring 300 enslaved people to freedom.

CONFIDENTIAL

SIDNEY REILLY
(1874–1925)

What was his claim to fame?

Known as the "ace of spies" and apparently the inspiration for James Bond, Sidney Reilly served as a key agent in the fight against Bolshevism (a type of extreme Russian communism).

Who did he work for?

Impressed by his language skills and willing to ignore his corrupt past, Britain's SIS (or MI6) recruited him in their drive to defeat Bolshevism in Europe.

What was his most-daring mission?

He led a top-secret but unsuccessful plot to overthrow the Russian Bolshevik government in 1918, and to assassinate their leader, Vladimir Lenin. He escaped to Finland, but the Russians caught and executed him years later.

URSULA KUCZYNSKI, or RUTH WERNER (1907–2000)

Which side did this spy work for?

She was born in Germany and became one of Russia's star agents. Do you remember the Cold War nuclear scientist Klaus Fuchs? Ursula was his handler (or officer in charge of agents on missions).

When did her spy career begin?

She was recruited in 1930, given the code name **Sonya**, and sent to Moscow to be trained in espionage and radio communications. She moved to Britain and became Fuchs's messenger. Strangely, she was allowed to escape from Britain the day before Fuchs's trial. As she wrote in her autobiography: "*Either it was stupidity on the part of MI5 . . . or they let me get away with it.*"

PEARL WITHERINGTON (1914–2008)

When did she operate?

A British spy, she parachuted into France during WWII with instructions sewn into the hem of her skirt. After her boss was caught by the Gestapo (the Nazis' secret police), Pearl became leader of her spy network.

What was her mission?

Disguised as a sales representative for a cosmetics firm, her job was to deliver messages, arms, and explosives around France. She led 1,500 to 3,500 resistance fighters, arranged weapons drops, distributed explosives, and planned her network's activities. She was so efficient that the Germans apparently offered a reward of one million francs for her capture.

ALDRICH AMES
(1941–)

Who is he?
A former CIA officer turned KGB agent.

Why did he become a double-agent?
Money! Soviet officials lured him with a promise of over $4 million, so he began to pass over stacks of classified documents and names of KGB **defectors** (former agents who switched sides).

How was he caught?
The CIA became suspicious of his lavish lifestyle, which included a new house and luxury car. They staked him out, and noticed that after dining with Soviet officials, Ames would get a few thousand dollars deposited in his bank account. He was finally arrested in 1994.

SPY TAILS

The espionage world is full of stories of human daring and deception. Read on to discover the part animals have played in the secret world of spies.

Spy animals! Are you joking?

It's true! Let's take **Project Acoustic Kitty** as an example. Back in the 1960s, the CIA spent $20 million developing technology that would allow cats to spy on the Russians. With a microphone implanted in its ear canal, and a transmitter at the base of its skull, the CIA hoped that this high-tech cat would stroll into the **Kremlin** (the citadel in Moscow that includes the Russian president's residence) and record, then transmit, secret conversations.

How did the experiment go? Did the cyborg cat prove to be the purr-fect spy?

Not exactly. The cat's test mission was to record the conversation of two Russian embassy officials in a Washington park. The cutting-edge cat chose to roam into the street, where it was flattened by a passing taxi!

Did the military give up on the idea of animal agents?

Not at all! The U.S. Navy has trained dolphins and sea lions to detect mines and enemy divers, and to recover equipment. The five marine mammal teams can be deployed around the world. Scientists have researched the possibility of **insect-cyborgs**. These bugs could be fitted with chemical sensors, cameras, or microphones to record secret chat. The biggest challenge? Protecting these ingenious insects from hungry birds!

Which animal has proved to be the most effective operator?
The pigeon! **GI Joe** was a WWII bird veteran who flew 20 miles (32 km) in 20 minutes to save over 1,000 lives in Calvi Vecchia, Italy. The American Air Force had planned a raid on the occupied village, but the British had liberated it from the Germans ahead of schedule. They were unable to radio through to the Americans to call off the raid, so they sent GI Joe as a last resort. He reached the base just as the planes were preparing for take-off. After the war, he was awarded the **Dickin Medal** for bravery alongside 31 fellow pigeons.

During the Cold War, ravens were trained to take undercover photographs and drop listening devices on windowsills.

What animal by-product is an underestimated spying essential?
Poop! A fake bird dropping splattered against a window can be a first-rate mini-listening device. The big blob can conceal a tiny transmitter, and the long drip hides an antenna.

Fake dog poop (code name **T-1151 Dog Poo Transmitter**) was used in the Vietnam War to signal when enemy supply movements took place overnight. This 4-inch (10 cm) long spy tool was small enough to be slipped into a pocket, and could lie without a trace of suspicion on the jungle floor.

Are there any secret agent animal stories left to be told?
In 2019, a baffling beluga whale surfaced in Norway. The unusually tame creature wore a harness that read "Equipment of St. Petersburg." As belugas are calm, trainable, and super-smart creatures, it was presumed that the beluga whale was on a Russian spying mission, but no one knows for sure.

RIGHT HERE! RIGHT NOW!

Let's get up-to-date with current spy operations! (Well, maybe not the top-secret ones!)

What are the main intelligence agencies around the world?
Take a look!

 USA Federal Bureau of Investigation (**FBI**) for domestic intelligence (inside the U.S.), Central Intelligence Agency (**CIA**) for foreign intelligence, National Security Agency (**NSA**) for cybersecurity, Defense Intelligence Agency (**DIA**) for military intelligence

 U.K. Security Service (also known as **MI5**) for domestic intelligence, Secret Intelligence Service (**SIS**, known as **MI6**) for international intelligence

 RUSSIA Federal Security Service (**FSB**) domestically; Foreign Intelligence Service (**SVR**) internationally—both were formerly the **KGB**.

 CHINA Ministry of State Security (**MSS**)

AUSTRALIA Australian Security Intelligence Organisation (**ASIO**) domestically; Australian Secret Intelligence Service (**ASIS**) internationally

 CANADA Royal Canadian Mounted Police (**RCMP** or the Mounties) domestically; Canadian Security Intelligence Service (**CSIS**) internationally

 NEW ZEALAND New Zealand Security Intelligence Service (**NZSIS**) for both domestic and foreign intelligence; Government Communications Security Bureau (**GCSB**) for cybersecurity

 FRANCE Directorate-General for Internal Security (**DGSI**) domestically; Directorate-General for External Security (**DGSE**) internationally

 INDIA Intelligence Bureau (**IB**) domestically; Research and Analysis Wing (**RAW**) internationally

 GERMANY Federal Office for the Protection of the Constitution (**BfV**) domestically; Federal Intelligence Service (**BND**) for foreign intelligence

 ISRAEL Israeli Security Agency (**ISA**) domestically; Mossad internationally

The United States, United Kingdom, Canada, New Zealand, and Australia are all allied together in a pact known as **Five Eyes (FIORC)**.

Are there different types of government spies?
Yes. Which of these roles would you apply for?

Intelligence Officer
You are highly trained in espionage and operate openly as a spy for an intelligence agency.

Undercover Intelligence Officer
You hide the fact that you're an intelligence service spy. You might be disguised as a journalist, a banker, a student, or other covers, and could take a false name and nationality.

Agent/Informant
You provide undercover information to intelligence officers and may have received some basic espionage lessons.

What are a secret agent's key skills?

If you fancy a career in an intelligence agency you should display the following know-how:

Languages

Do you speak a foreign language? How about learning Russian, Mandarin, or Arabic? A spy should be able to listen, translate, and analyze information, while showing an expert understanding of a country's history, culture, and politics.

Technology

Are you computer savvy? Intelligence agencies are on the lookout for investigators who can collect and analyze digital data to understand and disrupt threats from terrorists, spy networks, and cyber-attackers.

Science and Engineering

Do you think you could invent innovative gizmos to keep your intelligence agency ahead of the game? Keep concentrating in your science and math classes, as your expertise could help create the spy technology of the future!

Nonchalant Secrecy

To follow and observe targets in a mix of environments, you'll need to blend in. Do you have the patience and problem-solving skills needed to grab that key piece of intelligence from surveillance, a phone call, digital data, or human contact, without being detected?

What are the main priorities for intelligence agencies?

Government agents work hard to protect us from foreign espionage, terrorism, organized crime, weapons of mass destruction, and cyber-attacks. In the U.S., the job of the National Security Agency (NSA) is to defend the country's computer networks and assess the threat of cyber-attacks. They're also experts in making and breaking codes (cryptography).

It seems that cyber-attacks are getting more and more frequent.
Do spies just sit in front of a computer all day long?
Gathering cyber information is a popular intelligence method for the following reasons:

• It's cheaper than traditional methods.

• Because the agent is operating remotely, there is an added layer of security, and they can deny that they were snooping!

• The amount of data that can be retrieved is enormous!

However, the crucial component of espionage is still human contact between intelligence officer and agent.

So, human contact is still the number one spy technique, which is hard to believe in a world full of smartphones and computer data. How is this so? Let's take MI6 agent **Aimen Dean** (not his real name!), who was placed at the heart of the terrorist al-Qaida organization. He became close to the al-Qaida high command, and became one of their expert bomb-makers. He uncovered secret plans, and sent covert communications to foil plots and save hundreds of lives. He escaped death so often that his MI6 handlers called him "the spy with nine lives"!

CRYPTIC CODES

Secret codes have been used since the beginning of recorded history to protect information from falling into enemy hands!

How long have coded messages been around?
The earliest known coded writing is a set of **hieroglyphs** (*HI-roh-gliffs*, or writings in which words are depicted as letters) inscribed on the tomb of an ancient Egyptian noble almost four thousand years ago. These coded glyphs weren't hiding top-secret information, though. Instead, their meanings were probably meant to amuse tomb readers!

Did any ancient codes prove difficult to crack?
The **Caesar shift** (or **cipher**) is named after Roman Emperor **Julius Caesar**, who used it to encrypt his military plans. The concept is simple. You swap each letter in the alphabet by shifting it left or right by a set number of letters. It may be straightforward, but it took 800 years for codebreakers to crack it!

What makes someone a good codebreaker (or cryptanalyst)?
Are you investigative and inquisitive? Are you curious, methodical, rational, analytical, and logical? If you're the kind of person who never gives up on trying to solve a puzzle, then this could be the career for you!

How are coded messages sent?

Over the years, encrypted (hidden in code) information has been concealed in books, poems, music manuscripts, online photographs, hollow feather quills, and newspaper ads. In WWI, Native Americans, including members of the Choctaw people, worked as code talkers with the U.S. Army to send military plans in their tribal language by telephone. In World War II, Navajo code talkers continued this work. Meanwhile, in Nazi-occupied Belgium, a grandmother sat knitting at a window, observing passing trains. She added a bumpy stitch as one train went by, then left a hole to indicate that a different train had passed. She'd hand the fabric to a fellow Belgian spy as part of their effort to gather information on the German occupiers.

Who are the unsung heroines of the code-breaking community?

Women! In order to help crack the German Enigma code in WWII, 8,000 women worked in secret at Britain's Bletchley Park, making up 75 percent of the workforce. Over in the U.S., the cryptanalytic team working to crack Cold War Soviet spy communications was mainly female. Their numbers and math expertise helped to wrap up the VENONA project.

Elizebeth Friedman was one of the greatest codebreakers in history. She became the FBI's secret weapon by solving encrypted German messages in both world wars and, in between, helped put away three of Al Capone's gangsters!

SIGN ME UP!

Do you have what it takes to run a secret operation?
Here are some ways you could test out your spy skills!

What can I use to hide my secret messages?
Let's see if you can make your own invisible ink:

1 Squeeze half a lemon into a bowl.

2 Add a few drops of water to your lemon juice, then stir the mixture.

3 Use a cotton swab, feather, toothpick, or fountain pen to write a message on some paper.

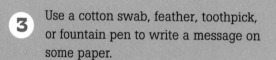

4 Let the invisible ink dry.

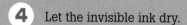

5 Hold the paper in front of a light bulb and see if you can read it!

How can I come up with a classified code?

Use the tips at the back of the book to write a secret sentence. Can your friends crack the code? You could try writing a message backwards so it can be read in a mirror!

What do I need to do to make a new identity?

What would your new name and background story be? Write down and memorize your personal details and practice your new signature. Can you think of a secret code name too?

NEW NAME IDEAS

JAMES POND	MR. C. CRET
RON FIDENTIAL	ANDY AGENT
MIKE MISSION	MR. S. P. EYE

How can I go undercover?

See if you can disguise yourself. Try blending in by wearing a hat and some dark, plain clothes, and hide your face with sunglasses. You could even practice talking in a different voice! Let your parents know what you're up to, though. They're your handlers, after all!

What should I put in my very own spy kit?

See if you can sign some forms or documents using your new name and identity. Carry some spy tools, including a magnifying glass, ink pad for fingerprints, notepad and pen (for taking down intel), and mini flashlight. Can you hide a secret message in an everyday object?

Where do secret agents go to school?

Spy High!

What else do I need to be a top spy?

A good spy needs to quickly read and recall critical information. Speaking of which...

So, you want to be a spy. Let's see if you can talk the talk! Memorize the following words, then close this book and see how many of them you can remember.

Asset
Someone who supplies intelligence to an agent

Brush Pass
A hurried meeting where an item is passed between an officer and an agent

Bugs
Hidden listening devices

Cobbler
A spy who forges passports, visas, and other documents

COMINT
Information gathered from transmissions (phone calls, text messages, online browsing, etc.)

Compromised
When your cover is blown!

Cover
A spy's identity while on a mission

Cryptanalyst
Someone who breaks codes and translates coded messages

Cryptology
The field of code-making and code-breaking

Dead Drop
A place where secret information is left for another agent to recover

Double Agent
Spies who seem to work for one country or organization but actually work for another, often the enemy of the people they pretend to work for

Enigma
The machine used by the Germans to send coded messages in WWII

Handler
An officer who's in charge of agents on spy missions

HUMINT
Information gathered from people (through interviews, casual interactions, etc.)

IMGINT
Information gathered from photos

Infiltrate
To sneak into

Intelligence
Another word for information

KGB
The Soviet Union's Cold War intelligence service

Legend
A spy's new background story

Mole
An agent sent to work in a rival intelligence agency

Naked
A spy on a mission with no cover or back-up

OSINT
Open-Source Intelligence—intelligence gathered from freely available sources (newspapers, TV broadcasts, government reports, etc.)

Plaintext
An original message before it was coded

RADINT
Information from radar images

Rolled-up
When a mission goes wrong and the spy is arrested

SIGINT
Information gathered from electronic sources in offices, satellites, ships, or planes. COMINT is a form of SIGINT (but not all SIGINT is COMINT).

Sleeper
An agent living as an everyday citizen in a target country until they're needed for a mission. When a sleeper takes on an active mission, this is called being activated.

Spymaster
The leader of a spy ring

Window Dressing
Extra elements in a spy's cover story to convince people that they're genuine

GET THE MESSAGE!

Any agent serious about spying should be able to send and decode secret messages. Here you can learn how to write your own codes, so let's get cracking!

How can I send a secret message without a pen and paper?

You can use **Morse code** to transmit messages as a series of beeps, taps, or flashes of light. Each message consists of **dashes** (long beeps or flashes—or, if you're tapping, a tap, followed by a pause) and **dots** (short beeps or flashes, or rapid taps). See if you can tap a message, or even flash one!

A lot of words and letters can sound the same over a crackly radio line. **How can I make sure my communication is received loud and clear?**

Use the **NATO phonetic alphabet**! Take a look at the chart below, then use the codes to say these words: STOP, ADVANCE, or RETREAT.

What is the simplest code for written reports?

You can give each letter a number based on the order of the alphabet. So for example, SEND/HELP would be 19-5-14-4/8-5-12-16.

That looks a little too easy! Can you recommend something more puzzling?

Try the **pigpen cipher**. This code swaps letters for symbols which are put on a grid like the ones shown here. Each letter is replaced by part of the image where it is found.

In this case, AGENT is ⌡ ⌐ ☐ ⊡ ⟩.

Now try some messages of your own.

CHECK OUT ALL OF THE FANTASTIC FACTS IN THIS SENSATIONAL SERIES!

100 Questions about the
Amazon Rainforest

100 Questions about Bugs

100 Questions about Colonial America

100 Questions about Dinosaurs

100 Questions about Extreme Weather

100 Questions about the Human Body

100 Questions about Oceans

100 Questions about Outer Space

100 Questions about Pirates

100 Questions about Rocks & Minerals

100 Questions about Sharks

100 Questions about Spies